KEYBOARD CHORDS
Deluxe

ISBN-13: 978-1-4234-1248-9
ISBN-10: 1-4234-1248-6

HAL•LEONARD®
CORPORATION

7777 W. BLUEMOUND RD. P.O. BOX 13819 MILWAUKEE, WI 53213

Visit Hal Leonard Online at
www.halleonard.com

CONTENTS

HOW TO USE THIS BOOK

Just a century ago, the average popular pianist had relatively few chords to worry about. Things have changed a great deal since then. Today, pianists must know how to construct an astounding assortment of chords. *Keyboard Chords Deluxe* is a valuable resource that will help in a number of ways:

- **as a chord dictionary**
  If you find a chord you're not familiar with in a piece of music, look it up in this book. If you compose music and create chords, this book will also help you to determine proper chord spelling.

- **as a fingering guide**
  If you're uncertain how to play a chord, just look at its accompanying photo. *Keyboard Chords Deluxe* takes the guesswork out of fingering by including a photo with every chord. You'll learn to play even the most advanced chords comfortably and naturally.

- **as a music reading tool**
  Observe each chord's notation on the staff as you learn to play it. Routine practice at this will improve your note reading and chord recognition skills tremendously.

- **as a resource for improvisers and non-pianists**
  A working knowledge of chords is essential to becoming an effective improviser. This book will help you to visualize possible note choices when improvising. Non-pianists may want to practice outlining the chords in the book as a way to better understand and conceptualize chords and harmony.

The Chord Chart on page 14 lists all the chord types included in *Keyboard Chords Deluxe*, in the order that they appear. you'll find that three-note chords (triads) appear first, then chords with four notes (seventh chords and sixth chords), and then more unusual chords (extensions, alterations, power chords, etc.). To find a chord, first notice its position on the chart, and then turn to the root of your choice (C, C♯/D♭, D, D♯/E♭, E, etc.) within the encyclopedia to locate the actual keyboard voicings.

To become more familiar with chord reading, here's a suggested practice routine.

1. **Learn triads.** Triads are three-note chords, and are the basis of keyboard harmony. Each triad is shown in three positions, or "inversions." Practice playing each of these up and down the keyboard.

2. **Learn seventh chords.** Seventh chords are a little more advanced. They consist of four notes, so each is shown in four positions or "inversions." Practice all positions.

3. **Try the rest.** If you're comfortable with triads and seventh chords, the remaining chords will come more easily. Extensions, alterations, and other chord types are all considered variations on basic triads or seventh chords.

BASIC CHORDS & INTERVALS

INTERVALS

Learning about intervals is a key element in learning how to construct chords. An *interval* describes the distance between two notes. For example, the distance from the note C to the note D is the interval of a "second." The distance from C to E is the interval of a "third," and so on. The reason intervals are so helpful is that, once you are comfortable visualizing intervals, it will be easy to construct any type of chord in any key. The real difficulty with intervals is determining whether an interval is major, minor, perfect, augmented, or diminished. It is important to understand that all similar chords contain similar intervals. For example, a C major triad contains a root, major third, and perfect fifth. Therefore, any major triad will contain a root, major third, and perfect fifth. Look at the example below. You will notice that, in a C major scale (or any other major scale), some intervals are *perfect* and some intervals are *major*. The reason for this is beyond the scope of this book. Suffice it to say that the intervals presented in this chapter are the results of many centuries of theory development. Just remember that fourths, fifths, and octaves are perfect, and all other intervals in a major scale are major.

A critical point to consider when learning about intervals is what happens when we alter an interval such as a perfect fifth. Consider the perfect fifth from the note C and G. What happens if we change the G to a G sharp? In this case, the interval becomes an *augmented* fifth. In other words, the space (or *interval*) between notes has been augmented, or increased. In this example, if the note G were a G flat, the interval would still be a fifth (C to G is always a fifth), but in this instance, the interval would be a *diminished* fifth. In other words, the interval between notes has been diminished, or decreased. The following example shows the terminology for altering major and perfect intervals. Note that the only difference between the two types of intervals is that when you make a major interval smaller, it becomes *minor*. When you make a perfect interval smaller, it becomes *diminished*. Other than this one distinction, the terminology for major and perfect intervals is the same. Note that the minor interval becomes diminished when made smaller.

Understanding the theory behind intervals is one thing, being able to utilize intervals in your playing is another. You may find it helpful to use some tricks to be able to comfortably visualize intervals. Begin by learning perfect fifths and major thirds. All other intervals can easily be related to these primary intervals. Regarding perfect fifths: with only two exceptions, both notes in a perfect fifth will share the same accidental. In the following example, you can see that the only fifths that don't follow this rule are B♭ to F and B to F♯.

Major thirds are also easy to find. To find a major third, count up two whole steps from any note. The following example illustrates common major thirds:

The following is a list of tricks to find common intervals:

- Major second: Count up one whole step from any note.
- Minor third: Lower the top note of any major third by one half step.
- Perfect fourth: Count down one whole step from the top note of any perfect fifth.
- Major sixth: Count up one whole step from any perfect fifth interval.
- Minor seventh: A whole step "shy" of an octave.
- Major seventh: A half step "shy" of an octave.
- Major ninth: Same note as a major second but an octave higher.
- Perfect eleventh: Same note as a perfect fourth but one octave higher.
- Major thirteenth: Same as a sixth but an octave higher.

As you can see, intervals are relatively easy to learn. The next step is to learn to construct chords using intervals.

TRIADS

Triads are chords consisting of three notes. The primary triads are *major, minor, diminished,* and *augmented.* Major and minor triads are most prevalent in music today. Note that in the figure below, both the major and minor triads contain a perfect fifth interval. The only difference is the interval of a third: major triads contain a major third, minor triads contain a minor third. As you can see, a diminished triad contains a minor third and a diminished fifth. The augmented triad contains a major third and an augmented fifth.

In the previous example, the root of each triad was the note C. This brings up an important point regarding construction of chords: Is the root always the lowest note? Unlike figured bass chord construction in traditional theory, the root may not always be the lowest note in popular music chord nomenclature. The root is always the lowest note in terms of chord construction (building a chord using intervals), but the root may not always be placed as the lowest note of the chord. Play the following chords:

In this example, the order of notes in the original C major triad has changed, but the chords still sound like the original C major chord. These new varieties of C major triads are called *inversions*. In the previous example, the triads may be described as *root position, first inversion*, and *second inversion*. **To invert any chord, raise the bottom note one octave or lower the top note one octave**. Generally, triads and seventh chords are the only chords that may be practically inverted. More complex chord inversions may be easily handled by adding notes to a simple triad or seventh chord inversion. As you will see, it is also common to omit some notes when inverting more complex chords.

There may be occasions where you would like to hear a chord with a tone other than the root in the bass register. In these cases, notate the name of the chord and use a slash to signify the bass note. C/G would be interpreted as a C major triad over the bass note G. Incidentally, notes other than chord tones may also be used. The chord F/G, for example, is common in popular music today. When inverting chords, be aware that the quality of chord may change if a note other than the root occurs in the bass register. A first inversion C major chord may sound different if placed below middle C on the piano. In this case, the lowest note (E) may start to sound like a root. The best way to determine the difference between a simple inversion and an actual change of chord type is through experimentation. Play chords and inversions in the lower register of the piano. You will start to get a sense of how range can alter the quality of a chord.

SEVENTH CHORDS

Seventh chords are common in many styles of music. The term "seventh chords" refers to triads that also contain an interval of a seventh. If you can construct basic triads, seventh chords are relatively easy to spell. Here are some common seventh chords:

Some tricks to remember:

- Major 7 chord: major triad and major seventh interval (Remember: a major seventh is a half step shy of an octave)
- Minor 7 chord: minor triad and minor seventh
- Major/minor 7:   minor triad and major seventh
- 7 chord: major triad with minor seventh interval
- Diminished 7:   diminished triad with diminished seventh interval (chord is constructed entirely from minor third intervals)

To this point, we have considered a variety of triads and seventh chords. Students would be advised to study construction of these chord types as well as inversions for the basic triads and seventh chords. Inversions for these chords may be found in the dictionary portion of *Keyboard Chords Deluxe*. In the next few pages, we will look at concepts relating to extensions and alterations.

EXTENSIONS AND ALTERATIONS

An *extension* refers to an interval greater than a seventh that is added to a chord. Examples of extensions are ninths, elevenths, and thirteenths. The term *alteration* refers to a chord where one of the primary intervals has been altered. We have already seen examples of altered chords. In the preceding section, a major triad had been altered to include an augmented (altered) fifth. The resulting chord was a C augmented (+) triad.

Questions often arise around the concept of extensions. An interval of a ninth is the same as a major second plus one octave. Why is it that ninth chords are not notated as "2nd" chords? The answer lies in the fact that our chord system is built around a concept of *tertian* harmony – chords built in thirds. A triad may contain a root, third, and fifth. A seventh chord contains a root, third, fifth, and seventh. A ninth chord contains a root, third, fifth, seventh, and ninth, and so on. Although there are a few exceptions, the basic rule is as follows: the higher the extension number, the more potential chord tones may be included in a voicing. To better understand this concept, visualize the difference between a C6 chord and a C13 chord. Although these chords might seem similar, the C6 chord is a simple major triad with an interval of a major sixth added. The C13 chord contains a minor seventh and major ninth interval in addition to a major triad. In the following example, note that no eleventh is present in the C13 chord. In the strictest technical sense the eleventh could be used. In this case, the reason for excluding it is simple – it sounds bad.

NINTH CHORDS

Ninth chords are chords that contain an interval of a ninth. In most cases, these chords are four-note seventh chords that also contain an interval of a major ninth. An important concept to remember when dealing with ninth chords is the following: major ninths are always added to chords unless otherwise specified. In the following example, notice how all of the example chords use the same major ninth interval – a D in this case.

There will be occasions where a minor or augmented ninth will be used, but this will always be specified with a qualifier such as + or ♯9, - or flat 9. Ninth chords can often be a point of confusion for students. With a chord such as a Cm9, you might expect that the ninth of this chord would be a minor ninth. In this case, the ninth is still a major ninth. Just remember that ninths are always major unless otherwise specified. An easy way to tell the type of underlying chord quality for any ninth chord is to replace 9 with 7. For example, an Fm9 is really an Fm7 with a major ninth added. A B9 is really a B7 with major ninth added.

ELEVENTH CHORDS

Eleventh chords are not as common as ninth chords. An easy way to find a perfect eleventh is to count down one whole step from the top note of a perfect fifth interval. An eleventh is the same as a perfect fourth plus an octave. It is interesting to note that the interval of an eleventh is typically altered. In common practice, the only time a perfect eleventh is added is over a minor seventh or minor ninth chord. A Cm11 chord, major ninth, and a perfect eleventh.

An augmented eleventh is more common, and is often in conjunction with major ninth chords and dominant ninth chords. Although the interval of an augmented eleventh is an enharmonic equivalent to a diminished fifth, in the following example, you can see that both a perfect fifth and augmented eleventh are used.

There is one other variety of eleventh chord that may cause some confusion. A C11 chord looks as if it may have evolved from a C7 or C9 chord. This is true, but unlike other examples to this point, the third is always omitted for this type of chord. A better way to describe this type of chord would be Gm7/C or C9sus.

THIRTEENTH CHORDS

The last type of extended chord we will look at are thirteenth chords. Like ninth chords, the interval of a thirteenth will always be a major thirteenth unless otherwise noted. The most common thirteenth chord is the "dominant thirteenth." A major thirteenth chord is also fairly common.

Notice the absence of an eleventh in these chords. It is customary to omit the eleventh on dominant or major thirteenth chords because the eleventh conflicts with the third.

OTHER CHORD TYPES

There are a great many chords that don't fit nicely into a major or minor category. Unlike major and minor triads and seventh chords, many of these chords may not be built in thirds. Sus4 and sus2 chords are two such examples. The sus4 chord has its roots in Renaissance harmony. At that point in time, *suspensions* were a common device. In a 4-3 suspension, an interval of a perfect fourth resolves to an interval of a third. In our modern equivalent, a perfect fourth is used instead of a major or minor third. The sus2 chord is similar. Here, a major second is used instead of a major or minor third.

ADD9 CHORDS

Intervals are sometimes added to a simple triad. In a C(add9) chord for example, an interval of a major ninth is added to a simple major triad. This chord is similar to a Csus2 with the exception that a C(add9) chord contains a major third.

SIXTH CHORDS

The interval of a sixth is another common interval that may be added to triads. This is so common that the "add6" qualifier is not needed. A C6 may be interpreted as a C major triad with a major sixth added. A Cm6 would be a C minor triad with major sixth added. A major ninth may also be added. Note that in all of the following chords, sixths and ninths are added to basic major or minor triads – no seventh is used.

POWER CHORDS

There is one other chord variety that should be mentioned in this section on chord construction. In some styles of popular music, it is customary to use "power chords" – chords that are not major or minor. In these cases, only a root and perfect fifth are used. A C5 chord, for example, would contain only the notes C and G.

To conclude this portion of the text, let's review some of the important concepts.
- Intervals are key to learning proper chord construction.
- Perfect fifths and major thirds are two helpful intervals – most other intervals can be found by counting up or down whole and half steps from these intervals.
- Triads are three-note chords.
- The most common triads are major, minor, diminished, and augmented.
- Seventh chords extend basic triads by adding the interval of a seventh. There are a great variety of seventh chords, but the most helpful to learn are: major 7, minor 7, 7, and diminished 7.
- Extensions may be added to seventh chords. Possible extension notes are the ninth, eleventh, and thirteenth.
- Chord tones may be altered. Augmented and diminished fifths are two examples of altered chord tones.

ADVANCED CHORD VOICINGS

Learning the notes of chords is only one facet of actually using chords effectively. Deciding how to "voice" or organize the notes of a given chord can be a daunting task. Many variables must be considered — range, spacing, complexity, and context. This section will provide some suggestions on common voicing techniques.

An important concept to understand when voicing chords is the fact that no specific order of notes is implied. For example, although a C9 chord does contain the note D (the ninth), the D may not actually be placed a ninth higher than the root. In some cases, it might be next to the root. The key here is to understand that a chord name describes the construction (in root position) of the chord. It does not imply a specific order of notes as they might actually be played.

OPEN VS. CLOSE

Close or "tight" voicings generally work fine in the mid and upper range of the piano, but as you move to the lower register the voicings will need to "open up." Below are a few common left hand structures. Notice how the interval between notes is fairly large in these examples.

In the next example, the right hand is voiced using "close" harmony. This works well because the right hand is in the middle register of the piano.

Is is important to avoid changing the quality of chord by placing notes other than the root in the bass register. In the following example, the first chord will sound like an Am7, not a C6. The reason for this is that the note A sounds like a root because of its position in the chord.

'A' sounds as root

DROP VOICINGS

One of the best ways to learn about voicing chords is to work with four-note seventh chords. *Keyboard Chords Deluxe* lists inversions for the primary seventh chords. Learn these inversions and you will find it is easy to voice more complex chords by adding tones to these primary inversions. The next few suggestions will apply to four-note voicings in the right hand. These suggestions are also applicable to mid-range left hand voicings as well.

- To add a ninth, drop the root.
- To add a thirteenth, drop the fifth.
- To add a ♯11, drop the fifth.

The term "drop" can mean two different things. You can drop the note to the left hand or you may even omit the note. The next example demonstrates this concept. Notice how each of the chords derives from a more basic seventh chord inversion.

The following demonstrates some possible voicings using a variety of notes in both the left and right hand. In these voicings, "dropped" notes are placed in the left hand.

Another approach to voicing a complex chord such as a ninth, eleventh, or thirteenth, is to begin with the third, fifth, seventh, and ninth in the right hand. This is always a good starting point. Extensions and alterations may be applied to this basic structure.

Another common structure are "drop 2" voicings. To make a drop 2, lower the second note from the top of any close position voicing one octave. Two inversions are particularly helpful: 3-7-9-5 and 7-3-5-9.

As you can see, learning to construct and voice chords is not an easy task. *The Picture Chord Encyclopedia* will be a valuable reference for learning chords. You will find an extensive listing of chords and inversions of primary triads and seventh chords. Learn the inversions, and it will be relatively easy to construct and voice even the most complex chord.

CHORD CHART

m = minor interval   **d = diminished interval**   **a = augmented interval**

All other intervals are major or perfect

Chord	Alternate Names	Spelling
C	CM, Cmaj., C △, Cmajor	1, 3, 5
Cm	Cmi., Cmin., C-	1, m3, 5
C+	Caug., C+5, C(♯5)	1, 3, ♯5
Cdim	C°, C diminished	1, m3, d5
Csus	Csus4	1, 4, 5
Csus2	C2	1, 2, 5
C6	Cmaj.6, Cadd6	1, 3, 5, 6
C(add2)	C(add9)	1, 2, 3, 5
Cmaj7	C △7, CM7, Cma7	1, 3, 5, 7
C7	none	1, 3, 5, m7
C7♭5	C7-5	1, 3, d5, m7
C7sus	C7sus4	1, 4, 5, m7
Cm(add2)	Cm2, C-2	1, 2, m3, 5
Cm6	Cm(add6), C-6	1, m3, 5, 6
Cm7	C-7, Cmi7, Cmin7	1, m3, 5, m7
Cm(maj7)	C-(△7), Cmi(ma7)	1, m3, 5, 7
Cm7♭5	CØ7, Cm7-5	1, m3, d5, m7
Cdim7	C°7	1, m3, d5, d7
C5	C(no 3rd)	1, 5
Cmaj7♯11	C △7(♯11)	1, 3, 5, 7, all
Cmaj9	C △9, CM9, Cma9	1, 3, 5, 7, 9
C7♯9	C7(+9)	1, 3, 5, m7, a9
C9	none	1, 3, 5, m7, 9
C11	C9sus4, Gm7/C	1, 5, m7, 9, 11
C13	none	1, 3, 5, m7, 9, 13
Cm9	C-9, Cmin9	1, m3, 5, m7, 9
Cm11	Cmin11, C-11	1, m3, 5, m7, 9, 11

C+   Root Position

Cdim   Root Position

C+   First Inversion

Cdim   First Inversion

C+   Second Inversion

Cdim   Second Inversion

Csus Root Position

Csus2 Root Position

Csus First Inversion

Csus2 First Inversion

Csus Second Inversion

Csus2 Second Inversion

C6   Root Position

C6   First Inversion

C6   Second Inversion

C6   Third Inversion

C(add2), C(add9) — Root Position

C(add2), C(add9) — First Inversion

C(add2), C(add9) — Second Inversion

C(add2), C(add9) — Third Inversion

Cmaj7
Root Position

Cmaj7
First Inversion

C E G B

E G B C

Cmaj7
Second Inversion

G B C E

Cmaj7
Third Inversion

B C E G

C7 Root Position

C   E   G   B♭

C7 First Inversion

E   G   B♭   C

C7 Second Inversion

G   B♭   C   E

C7 Third Inversion

B♭   C   E   G

C7♭5   Root Position

C7♭5   First Inversion

C7♭5   Second Inversion

C7♭5   Third Inversion

C7sus Root Position

C7sus First Inversion

C7sus Second Inversion

C7sus Third Inversion

Cm(add2), Cm(add9) Root Position

Cm(add2), Cm(add9) First Inversion

Cm(add2), Cm(add9) Second Inversion

Cm(add2), Cm(add9) Third Inversion

Cm6 Root Position

C E♭ G A

Cm6 First Inversion

E♭ G A C

Cm6 Second Inversion

G A C E♭

Cm6 Third Inversion

A C E♭ G

Cm7 Root Position

Cm7 First Inversion

Cm7 Second Inversion

Cm7 Third Inversion

Cm(maj7)   Root Position

C E♭   G   B

Cm(maj7)   First Inversion

E♭   G B C

Cm(maj7)   Second Inversion

G B C E♭

Cm(maj7)   Third Inversion

B C E♭   G

Cm7♭5 Root Position

C   E♭   G♭   B♭

Cm7♭5 First Inversion

E♭   G♭   B♭   C

Cm7♭5 Second Inversion

G♭   B♭   C   E♭

Cm7♭5 Third Inversion

B♭   C   E♭   G♭

Cdim7 Root Position

Cdim7 First Inversion

Cdim7 Second Inversion

Cdim7 Third Inversion

C5

C7#9

Cmaj7#11

C9

Cmaj9

C11, C9(sus4)

C13

Cm9

Cm11

C# — Root Position

C#m — Root Position

C# — First Inversion

C#m — First Inversion

C# — Second Inversion

C#m — Second Inversion

C#+ Root Position

C#dim Root Position

C#+ First Inversion

C#dim First Inversion

C#+ Second Inversion

C#dim Second Inversion

C#sus Root Position

C#sus2 Root Position

C#
Db

C#sus First Inversion

C#sus2 First Inversion

C#sus Second Inversion

C#sus2 Second Inversion

C#6 Root Position

C# E# G# A#

C#6 First Inversion

E# G# A# C#

C#6 Second Inversion

G# A# C# E#

C#6 Third Inversion

A# C# E# G#

C#(add2), C#(add9) Root Position

C# D# E# G#

C#(add2), C#(add9) First Inversion

D# E# G#   C#

C#(add2), C#(add9) Second Inversion

E# G#   C# D#

C#(add2), C#(add9) Third Inversion

G#   C# D# E#

C#maj7 Root Position

C#maj7 First Inversion

C#maj7 Second Inversion

C#maj7 Third Inversion

C#7 Root Position

C#7 First Inversion

C#/D♭

C#7 Second Inversion

C#7 Third Inversion

C#7♭5 Root Position

C# E# G B

C#7♭5 First Inversion

E# G B C#

C#7♭5 Second Inversion

G B C# E#

C#7♭5 Third Inversion

B C# E# G

C#7sus Root Position

C#7sus First Inversion

C#
Db

C#7sus Second Inversion

C#7sus Third Inversion

C♯m(add2), C♯m(add9) Root Position

C♯m(add2), C♯m(add9) First Inversion

C♯m(add2), C♯m(add9) Second Inversion

C♯m(add2), C♯m(add9) Third Inversion

C♯m6   Root Position

C♯   E   G♯ A♯

C♯m6   First Inversion

E   G♯ A♯   C♯

C♯m6   Second Inversion

G♯ A♯   C♯   E

C♯m6   Third Inversion

A♯   C♯   E   G♯

C#m7 Root Position

C# E G# B

C#m7 First Inversion

E G# B C#

C#m7 Second Inversion

G# B C# E

C#m7 Third Inversion

B C# E G#

C#m(maj7) Root Position

C#m(maj7) First Inversion

C#m(maj7) Second Inversion

C#m(maj7) Third Inversion

C#m7♭5 Root Position

C#m7♭5 First Inversion

C#m7♭5 Second Inversion

C#m7♭5 Third Inversion

C#dim7 Root Position

C#dim7 First Inversion

C#dim7 Second Inversion

C#dim7 Third Inversion

C#5

C#7#9

C#maj7#11

C#9

C#maj9

C#11, C#9(sus4)

C#13

C# E# G# B D# A#

C#m9

C# E G# B D#

C#m11

C# E G# B D# F#

D — Root Position

Dm — Root Position

D — First Inversion

Dm — First Inversion

D — Second Inversion

Dm — Second Inversion

D+ Root Position

Ddim Root Position

D+ First Inversion

Ddim First Inversion

D+ Second Inversion

Ddim Second Inversion

Dsus   Root Position

Dsus2   Root Position

Dsus   First Inversion

Dsus2   First Inversion

Dsus   Second Inversion

Dsus2   Second Inversion

D6   Root Position

D6   First Inversion

D6   Second Inversion

D6   Third Inversion

D(add2), D(add9) Root Position

D(add2), D(add9) First Inversion

D(add2), D(add9) Second Inversion

D(add2), D(add9) Third Inversion

Dmaj7 Root Position

Dmaj7 First Inversion

Dmaj7 Second Inversion

Dmaj7 Third Inversion

D7   Root Position

D7   First Inversion

D7   Second Inversion

D7   Third Inversion

D7♭5   Root Position

D7♭5   First Inversion

D

D7♭5   Second Inversion

D7♭5   Third Inversion

D7sus Root Position

D7sus First Inversion

D7sus Second Inversion

D7sus Third Inversion

Dm(add2), Dm(add9) Root Position

D E F A

Dm(add2), Dm(add9) First Inversion

E F A D

D

Dm(add2), Dm(add9) Second Inversion

F A D E

Dm(add2), Dm(add9) Third Inversion

A D E F

Dm6 Root Position

Dm6 First Inversion

Dm6 Second Inversion

Dm6 Third Inversion

Dm7 Root Position

Dm7 First Inversion

Dm7 Second Inversion

Dm7 Third Inversion

Dm(maj7) Root Position

Dm(maj7) First Inversion

Dm(maj7) Second Inversion

Dm(maj7) Third Inversion

Dm7♭5 Root Position

Dm7♭5 First Inversion

Dm7♭5 Second Inversion

Dm7♭5 Third Inversion

Ddim7 Root Position

D F A♭ C♭

Ddim7 First Inversion

F A♭ C♭ D

Ddim7 Second Inversion

A♭ C♭ D F

Ddim7 Third Inversion

C♭ D F A♭

D5

D7#9

Dmaj7#11

D9

Dmaj9

D11, D9(sus4)

D

D13

Dm9

Dm11

E♭ — Root Position

E♭m — Root Position

E♭ — First Inversion

E♭m — First Inversion

E♭

E♭ — Second Inversion

E♭m — Second Inversion

E♭+ Root Position

E♭ G B

E♭dim Root Position

E♭ G♭ A
(B♭♭)

E♭+ First Inversion

G B E♭

E♭dim First Inversion

G♭ A E♭
(B♭♭)

E♭+ Second Inversion

B E♭ G

E♭dim Second Inversion

A E♭ G♭
(B♭♭)

E♭sus — Root Position

E♭sus2 — Root Position

E♭sus — First Inversion

E♭sus2 — First Inversion

E♭sus — Second Inversion

E♭sus2 — Second Inversion

E♭

E♭6   Root Position

E♭6   First Inversion

E♭6   Second Inversion

E♭6   Third Inversion

E♭(add2), E♭(add9)   Root Position

E♭ F G B♭

E♭(add2), E♭(add9)   First Inversion

F G B♭ E♭

E♭

E♭(add2), E♭(add9)   Second Inversion

G B♭ E♭ F

E♭(add2), E♭(add9)   Third Inversion

B♭ E♭ F G

E♭maj7 Root Position

E♭maj7 First Inversion

E♭maj7 Second Inversion

E♭maj7 Third Inversion

E♭7 — Root Position

Eb   G   Bb   Db

E♭7 — First Inversion

G   Bb   Db Eb

E♭

E♭7 — Second Inversion

Bb   Db Eb   G

E♭7 — Third Inversion

Db Eb   G   Bb

E♭7♭5 Root Position

E♭   G   A   D♭
       (B♭♭)

E♭7♭5 First Inversion

G   A   D♭ E♭
   (B♭♭)

E♭7♭5 Second Inversion

A   D♭ E♭   G
(B♭♭)

E♭7♭5 Third Inversion

D♭ E♭   G   A
               (B♭♭)

E♭7sus Root Position

E♭7sus First Inversion

E♭7sus Second Inversion

E♭7sus Third Inversion

E♭

E♭m(add2), E♭m(add9) Root Position

E♭m(add2), E♭m(add9) First Inversion

E♭m(add2), E♭m(add9) Second Inversion

E♭m(add2), E♭m(add9) Third Inversion

E♭m6 Root Position

E♭m6 First Inversion

E♭m6 Second Inversion

E♭m6 Third Inversion

E♭m7 Root Position

E♭m7 First Inversion

E♭m7 Second Inversion

E♭m7 Third Inversion

E♭m(maj7) Root Position

E♭m(maj7) First Inversion

E♭m(maj7) Second Inversion

E♭m(maj7) Third Inversion

E♭m7♭5 Root Position

E♭m7♭5 First Inversion

E♭m7♭5 Second Inversion

E♭m7♭5 Third Inversion

E♭dim7 Root Position

E♭ G♭ A   C
      (B♭♭)(D♭♭)

E♭dim7 First Inversion

G♭ A   C   E♭
   (B♭♭)(D♭♭)

E♭

E♭dim7 Second Inversion

A   C   E♭ G♭
(B♭♭)(D♭♭)

E♭dim7 Third Inversion

C   E♭ G♭ A
(D♭♭)   (B♭♭)

E♭5

E♭7#9

E♭maj7#11

E♭9

E♭maj9

E♭11, E♭9(sus4)

E♭13

E♭m9

E♭m11

E♭

E+ — Root Position

Edim — Root Position

E+ — First Inversion

Edim — First Inversion

E+ — Second Inversion

Edim — Second Inversion

E

Esus Root Position

Esus2 Root Position

Esus First Inversion

Esus2 First Inversion

Esus Second Inversion

Esus2 Second Inversion

E6   Root Position

E   G#   B   C#

E6   First Inversion

G#   B   C#   E

E

E6   Second Inversion

B   C#   E   G#

E6   Third Inversion

C#   E   G#   B

E(add2), E(add9) Root Position

E   F# G#   B

E(add2), E(add9) First Inversion

F# G#   B   E

E(add2), E(add9) Second Inversion

G#   B   E   F#

E(add2), E(add9) Third Inversion

B   E   F# G#

Emaj7 Root Position

E G# B D#

Emaj7 First Inversion

G# B D#E

E

Emaj7 Second Inversion

B D#E G#

Emaj7 Third Inversion

D#E G# B

E7 Root Position

E G♯ B D

E7 First Inversion

G♯ B D E

E7 Second Inversion

B D E G♯

E7 Third Inversion

D E G♯ B

E7♭5 Root Position

E7♭5 First Inversion

E7♭5 Second Inversion

E7♭6 Third Inversion

E

E7sus Root Position

E   A   B   D

E7sus First Inversion

A   B   D   E

E7sus Second Inversion

B   D   E   A

E7sus Third Inversion

D   E   A   B

Em(add2), Em(add9) Root Position

Em(add2), Em(add9) First Inversion

E

Em(add2), Em(add9) Second Inversion

Em(add2), Em(add9) Third Inversion

Em6 Root Position

Em6 First Inversion

Em6 Second Inversion

Em6 Third Inversion

Em7 Root Position

E G B D

Em7 First Inversion

G B D E

E

Em7 Second Inversion

B D E G

Em7 Third Inversion

D E G B

Em(maj7) Root Position

E   G   B   D#

Em(maj7) First Inversion

G   B   D#E

Em(maj7) Second Inversion

B   D#E   G

Em(maj7) Third Inversion

D#E   G   B

Em7♭5 Root Position

Em7♭5 First Inversion

Em7♭5 Second Inversion

Em7♭5 Third Inversion

E

Edim7 Root Position

E G B♭ D♭

Edim7 First Inversion

G B♭ D♭ E

Edim7 Second Inversion

B♭ D♭ E G

Edim7 Third Inversion

D♭ E G B♭

E5

E   B

E7#9

E   G#   B   D   G
(Fx)

Emaj7#11

E   G#   B   D#   A#

E9

E   G#   B   D   F#

Emaj9

E   G#   B   D#   F#

E11, E9(sus4)

E   B   D   F#   A

E

E13

Em9

Em11

F

Root Position

F

First Inversion

F

Second Inversion

Fm

Root Position

Fm

First Inversion

Fm

Second Inversion

F+ Root Position

Fdim Root Position

F+ First Inversion

Fdim First Inversion

F+ Second Inversion

Fdim Second Inversion

Fsus Root Position

Fsus2 Root Position

Fsus First Inversion

Fsus2 First Inversion

F

Fsus Second Inversion

Fsus2 Second Inversion

F6   Root Position

F6   First Inversion

F6   Second Inversion

F6   Third Inversion

F(add2), F(add9) Root Position

F G A   C

F(add2), F(add9) First Inversion

G A   C   F

F

F(add2), F(add9) Second Inversion

A   C   F G

F(add2), F(add9) Third Inversion

C   F G A

Fmaj7 Root Position

Fmaj7 First Inversion

Fmaj7 Second Inversion

Fmaj7 Third Inversion

F7♭5 Root Position

F7♭5 First Inversion

F7♭5 Second Inversion

F7♭5 Third Inversion

F7sus Root Position

F   B♭   C   E♭

F7sus First Inversion

B♭   C   E♭   F

F7sus Second Inversion

C   E♭   F   B♭

F7sus Third Inversion

E♭   F   B♭   C

F

Fm(add2), Fm(add9) Root Position

Fm(add2), Fm(add9) First Inversion

Fm(add2), Fm(add9) Second Inversion

Fm(add2), Fm(add9) Third Inversion

Fm6   Root Position

F   A♭   C   D

Fm6   First Inversion

A♭   C   D   F

F

Fm6   Second Inversion

C   D   F   A♭

Fm6   Third Inversion

D   F   A♭   C

Fm7   Root Position

Fm7   First Inversion

Fm7   Second Inversion

Fm7   Third Inversion

Fm(maj7) Root Position

Fm(maj7) First Inversion

F

Fm(maj7) Second Inversion

Fm(maj7) Third Inversion

114

Fm7♭5 Root Position

F A♭ C♭ E♭

Fm7♭5 First Inversion

A♭ C♭ E♭ F

Fm7♭5 Second Inversion

C♭ E♭ F A♭

Fm7♭5 Third Inversion

E♭ F A♭ C♭

Fdim7 Root Position

Fdim7 First Inversion

Fdim7 Second Inversion

Fdim7 Third Inversion

F

F5

F7#9

Fmaj7#11

F9

Fmaj9

F11, F9(sus4)

F13

Fm9

Fm11

F#+ — Root Position

F# A# D
(C×)

F#dim — Root Position

F# A C

F#+ — First Inversion

A# D F#
(C×)

F#dim — First Inversion

A C F#

F#+ — Second Inversion

D F# A#
(C×)

F#dim — Second Inversion

C F# A

F#sus   Root Position

F#sus2   Root Position

F#sus   First Inversion

F#sus2   First Inversion

F#sus   Second Inversion

F#sus2   Second Inversion

F#6   Root Position

F#6   First Inversion

F#6   Second Inversion

F#6   Third Inversion

F#
G

F#(add2), F#(add9) Root Position

F# G# A#   C#

F#(add2), F#(add9) First Inversion

G# A#   C#   F#

F#(add2), F#(add9) Second Inversion

A#   C#   F# G#

F#(add2), F#(add9) Third Inversion

C#   F# G# A#

F#maj7 Root Position

F#maj7 First Inversion

F#maj7 Second Inversion

F#maj7 Third Inversion

F#
G♭

F#7   Root Position

F#   A#   C#   E

F#7   First Inversion

A#   C#   E   F#

F#7   Second Inversion

C#   E   F#   A#

F#7   Third Inversion

E   F#   A#   C#

F#7b5 Root Position

F# A# C E

F#7b5 First Inversion

A# C E F#

F#7b5 Second Inversion

C E F# A#

F#7b5 Third Inversion

E F# A# C

F#
Gb

F#7sus Root Position

F# B C# E

F#7sus First Inversion

B C# E F#

F#7sus Second Inversion

C# E F# B

F#7sus Third Inversion

E F# B C#

F#m(add2), F#m(add9) Root Position

F#m(add2), F#m(add9) First Inversion

F#m(add2), F#m(add9) Second Inversion

F#m(add2), F#m(add9) Third Inversion

F#m6 Root Position

F# A C# D#

F#m6 First Inversion

A C# D# F#

F#m6 Second Inversion

C# D# F# A

F#m6 Third Inversion

D# F# A C#

F#m7 Root Position

F#m7 First Inversion

F#m7 Second Inversion

F#m7 Third Inversion

F#m(maj7) Root Position

F# A C# E#

F#m(maj7) First Inversion

A C# E# F#

F#m(maj7) Second Inversion

C# E# F# A

F#m(maj7) Third Inversion

E# F# A C#

F#m7♭5 Root Position

F# A C E

F#m7♭5 First Inversion

A C E F#

F#m7♭5 Second Inversion

C E F# A

F#m7♭5 Third Inversion

E F# A C

F#dim7 Root Position

F#dim7 First Inversion

F#dim7 Second Inversion

F#dim7 Third Inversion

F#5

F#maj7#11

F#maj9

F#7#9

F#9

F#11, F#9(sus4)

F#13

F# A# C# E   G#   D#

F#m9

F# A   C# E   G#

F#m11

F# A   C# E   G# B

G Root Position

Gm Root Position

G First Inversion

Gm First Inversion

G

G Second Inversion

Gm Second Inversion

G+ Root Position

Gdim Root Position

G+ First Inversion

Gdim First Inversion

G+ Second Inversion

Gdim Second Inversion

Gsus Root Position

Gsus2 Root Position

Gsus First Inversion

Gsus2 First Inversion

Gsus Second Inversion

Gsus2 Second Inversion

G

G6 Root Position

G6 First Inversion

G6 Second Inversion

G6 Third Inversion

G(add2), G(add9)   Root Position

G(add2), G(add9)   First Inversion

G(add2), G(add9)   Second Inversion

G(add2), G(add9)   Third Inversion

Gmaj7 Root Position

G B D F#

Gmaj7 First Inversion

B D F#G

Gmaj7 Second Inversion

D F#G B

Gmaj7 Third Inversion

F#G B D

G7   Root Position

G B D F

G7   First Inversion

B D F G

C7   Second Inversion

D F G B

G7   Third Inversion

F G B D

G

G7♭5   Root Position

G7♭5   First Inversion

G7♭5   Second Inversion

G7♭5   Third Inversion

G7sus Root Position

G7sus First Inversion

G7sus Second Inversion

G7sus Third Inversion

G

144

Gm(add2), Gm(add9) Root Position

Gm(add2), Gm(add9) First Inversion

Gm(add2), Gm(add9) Second Inversion

Gm(add2), Gm(add9) Third Inversion

Gm6 Root Position

Gm6 First Inversion

Gm6 Second Inversion

Gm6 Third Inversion

G

Gm7 Root Position

Gm7 First Inversion

Gm7 Second Inversion

Gm7 Third Inversion

Gm(maj7) Root Position

G Bb D F#

Gm(maj7) First Inversion

Bb D F#G

Gm(maj7) Second Inversion

D F#G Bb

Gm(maj7) Third Inversion

F#G Bb D

G

Gm7♭5 Root Position

G B♭ D♭ F

Gm7♭5 First Inversion

B♭ D♭ F G

Gm7♭5 Second Inversion

D♭ F G B♭

Gm7♭5 Third Inversion

F G B♭ D♭

Gdim7 Root Position

Gdim7 First Inversion

Gdim7 Second Inversion

Gdim7 Third Inversion

G

G5

G7#9

Gmaj7#11

G9

Gmaj9

G11, G9(sus4)

G13

Gm9

Gm11

A♭+ Root Position

A♭dim Root Position

A♭+ First Inversion

A♭dim First Inversion

A♭+ Second Inversion

A♭dim Second Inversion

A♭SUS Root Position

A♭SUS2 Root Position

A♭SUS First Inversion

A♭SUS2 First Inversion

A♭SUS Second Inversion

A♭SUS2 Second Inversion

A♭6   Root Position

A♭6   First Inversion

A♭6   Second Inversion

A♭6   Third Inversion

A♭

A♭(add2), A♭(add9) Root Position

A♭(add2), A♭(add9) First Inversion

A♭(add2), A♭(add9) Second Inversion

A♭(add2), A♭(add9) Third Inversion

A♭maj7 Root Position

A♭maj7 First Inversion

A♭maj7 Second Inversion

A♭maj7 Third Inversion

A♭

A♭7   Root Position

A♭   C   E♭   G♭

A♭7   First Inversion

C   E♭   G♭ A♭

A♭7   Second Inversion

E♭   G♭ A♭   C

A♭7   Third Inversion

G♭ A♭   C   E♭

A♭7♭5 Root Position

A♭7♭5 First Inversion

A♭7♭5 Second Inversion

A♭7♭5 Third Inversion

A♭

A♭7sus Root Position

A♭7sus First Inversion

A♭7sus Second Inversion

A♭7sus Third Inversion

A♭m(add2), A♭m(add9) Root Position

A♭m(add2), A♭m(add9) First Inversion

A♭m(add2), A♭m(add9) Second Inversion

A♭m(add2), A♭m(add9) Third Inversion

A♭

A♭m6   Root Position

A♭   C♭   E♭   F

A♭m6   First Inversion

C♭   E♭   F   A♭

A♭m6   Second Inversion

E♭   F   A♭   C♭

A♭m6   Third Inversion

F   A♭   C♭   E♭

A♭m7 Root Position

A♭ C♭ E♭ G♭

A♭m7 First Inversion

C♭ E♭ G♭ A♭

A♭m7 Second Inversion

E♭ G♭ A♭ C♭

A♭m7 Third Inversion

G♭ A♭ C♭ E♭

A♭

A♭m(maj7) Root Position

A♭ C♭ E♭ G

A♭m(maj7) First Inversion

C♭ E♭ G A♭

A♭m(maj7) Second Inversion

E♭ G A♭ C♭

A♭m(maj7) Third Inversion

G A♭ C♭ E♭

A♭m7♭5 Root Position

A♭ C♭ D
(E♭) G♭

A♭m7♭5 First Inversion

C♭ D G♭ A♭
(E♭)

A♭m7♭5 Second Inversion

D G♭ A♭ C♭
(E♭)

A♭m7♭5 Third Inversion

G♭ A♭ C♭ D
(E♭)

A♭

A♭dim7 Root Position

A♭dim7 First Inversion

A♭dim7 Second Inversion

A♭dim7 Third Inversion

A♭5

A♭maj7♯11

A♭maj9

A♭7♯9

A♭9

A♭11, A♭9(sus4)

A♭

A♭13

A♭m9

A♭m11

A — Root Position

A C# E

Am — Root Position

A C E

A — First Inversion

C# E A

Am — First Inversion

C E A

A — Second Inversion

E A C#

Am — Second Inversion

E A C

A

Asus Root Position

Asus2 Root Position

Asus First Inversion

Asus2 First Inversion

Asus Second Inversion

Asus2 Second Inversion

A

172

A6 Root Position

A C# E F#

A6 First Inversion

C# E F# A

A6 Second Inversion

E F# A C#

A6 Third Inversion

F# A C# E

A(add2), A(add9) — Root Position

A(add2), A(add9) — First Inversion

A(add2), A(add9) — Second Inversion

A(add2), A(add9) — Third Inversion

A

Amaj7 Root Position

A   C#   E   G#

Amaj7 First Inversion

C#   E   G#A

Amaj7 Second Inversion

E   G#A   C#

Amaj7 Third Inversion

G#A   C#   E

A7   Root Position

A   C#   E   G

A7   First Inversion

C#   E   G   A

A7   Second Inversion

E   G   A   C#

A7   Third Inversion

G   A   C#   E

A

A7♭5 Root Position

A C# E♭ G

A7♭5 First Inversion

C# E♭ G A

A7♭5 Second Inversion

E♭ G A C#

A7♭5 Third Inversion

G A C# E♭

A7sus Root Position

A7sus First Inversion

A7sus Second Inversion

A7sus Third Inversion

A

Am(add2), Am(add9) Root Position

Am(add2), Am(add9) First Inversion

Am(add2), Am(add9) Second Inversion

Am(add2), Am(add9) Third Inversion

Am6 Root Position

Am6 First Inversion

Am6 Second Inversion

Am6 Third Inversion

A

Am7 Root Position

Am7 First Inversion

Am7 Second Inversion

Am7 Third Inversion

Am(maj7) Root Position

A   C   E   G#

Am(maj7) First Inversion

C   E   G#A

Am(maj7) Second Inversion

E   G#A   C

Am(maj7) Third Inversion

G#A   C   E

A

Am7♭5 Root Position

Am7♭5 First Inversion

Am7♭5 Second Inversion

Am7♭5 Third Inversion

Adim7 Root Position

A   C   Eb   Gb

Adim7 First Inversion

C   Eb   Gb   A

Adim7 Second Inversion

Eb   G   A   C

Adim7 Third Inversion

Gb   A   C   Eb

A

A5

A7#9

Amaj7#11

A9

Amaj9

A11, A9(sus4)

A13

Am9

Am11

A

B♭ Root Position

B♭m Root Position

B♭ First Inversion

B♭m First Inversion

B♭ Second Inversion

B♭m Second Inversion

B♭+ Root Position

B♭   D   F#

B♭dim Root Position

B♭   D♭   F♭

B♭+ First Inversion

D   F#   B♭

B♭dim First Inversion

D♭   F♭   B♭

B♭+ Second Inversion

F#   B♭   D

B♭dim Second Inversion

F♭   B♭   D♭

B♭

B♭SUS Root Position

Bb   Eb F

B♭SUS2 Root Position

Bb   C   F

B♭SUS First Inversion

Eb F   Bb

B♭SUS2 First Inversion

C   F   Bb

B♭SUS Second Inversion

F   Bb   Eb

B♭SUS2 Second Inversion

F   Bb   C

B♭6 Root Position

B♭6 First Inversion

B♭6 Second Inversion

B♭6 Third Inversion

B♭

B♭(add2), B♭(add9) Root Position

B♭(add2), B♭(add9) First Inversion

B♭(add2), B♭(add9) Second Inversion

B♭(add2), B♭(add9) Third Inversion

B♭maj7 Root Position

B♭maj7 First Inversion

B♭maj7 Second Inversion

B♭maj7 Third Inversion

B♭7   Root Position

B♭   D   F   A♭

B♭7   First Inversion

D   F   A♭   B♭

B♭7   Second Inversion

F   A♭   B♭   D

B♭7   Third Inversion

A♭   B♭   D   F

B♭7♭5 Root Position

B♭7♭5 First Inversion

B♭7♭5 Second Inversion

B♭7♭5 Third Inversion

B♭

B♭7sus Root Position

B♭7sus First Inversion

B♭   E♭   F   A♭

E♭   F   A♭   B♭

B♭7sus Second Inversion

B♭7sus Third Inversion

F   A♭   B♭   E♭

A♭   B♭   E♭   F

B♭m(add2), B♭m(add9) Root Position

B♭m(add2), B♭m(add9) First Inversion

B♭m(add2), B♭m(add9) Second Inversion

B♭m(add2), B♭m(add9) Third Inversion

B♭

B♭m6 Root Position

B♭m6 First Inversion

B♭m6 Second Inversion

B♭m6 Third Inversion

B♭m7 Root Position

B♭ D♭ F A♭

B♭m7 First Inversion

D♭ F A♭ B♭

B♭m7 Second Inversion

F A♭ B♭ D♭

B♭m7 Third Inversion

A♭ B♭ D♭ F

B♭

B♭m(maj7) Root Position

B♭   D♭   F   A

B♭m(maj7) First Inversion

D♭   F   A B♭

B♭m(maj7) Second Inversion

F   A B♭   D♭

B♭m(maj7) Third Inversion

A B♭   D♭   F

B♭m7♭5 Root Position

B♭ D♭ F♭ A♭

B♭m7♭5 First Inversion

D♭ F♭ A♭ B♭

B♭m7♭5 Second Inversion

F♭ A♭ B♭ D♭

B♭m7♭5 Third Inversion

A♭ B♭ D♭ F♭

B♭

B♭dim7 Root Position

B♭dim7 First Inversion

B♭dim7 Second Inversion

B♭dim7 Third Inversion

B♭5

B♭7#9

B♭maj7#11

B♭9

B♭maj9

B♭11, B♭9(sus4)

B♭

B♭13

B♭m9

B♭m11

B — Root Position

Bm — Root Position

B — First Inversion

Bm — First Inversion

B — Second Inversion

Bm — Second Inversion

B

Bsus Root Position

Bsus2 Root Position

Bsus First Inversion

Bsus2 First Inversion

Bsus Second Inversion

Bsus2 Second Inversion

B

B6 — Root Position

B6 — First Inversion

B6 — Second Inversion

B6 — Third Inversion

207

B(add2), B(add9) — Root Position

B(add2), B(add9) — First Inversion

B(add2), B(add9) — Second Inversion

B(add2), B(add9) — Third Inversion

B

Bmaj7 Root Position

B D♯ F♯ A♯

Bmaj7 First Inversion

D♯ F♯ A♯ B

Bmaj7 Second Inversion

F♯ A♯ B D♯

Bmaj7 Third Inversion

A♯ B D♯ F♯

B7 — Root Position

B   D♯   F♯   A

B7 — First Inversion

D♯   F♯   A   B

B7 — Second Inversion

F♯   A   B   D♯

B7 — Third Inversion

A   B   D♯   F♯

B

B7♭5 Root Position

B   D♯   F   A

B7♭5 First Inversion

D♯   F   A   B

B7♭5 Second Inversion

F   A   B   D♯

B7♭5 Third Inversion

A   B   D♯   F

B7sus Root Position

B   E   F♯   A

B7sus First Inversion

E   F♯   A   B

B7sus Second Inversion

F♯   A   B   E

B7sus Third Invoroion

A   B   E   F♯

B

Bm(add2), Bm(add9) Root Position

Bm(add2), Bm(add9) First Inversion

Bm(add2), Bm(add9) Second Inversion

Bm(add2), Bm(add9) Third Inversion

Bm6 Root Position

B D F♯ G♯

Bm6 First Inversion

D F♯ G♯ B

Bm6 Second Inversion

F♯ G♯ B D

Bm6 Third Inversion

G♯ B D F♯

B

Bm7 Root Position

B D F♯ A

Bm7 First Inversion

D F♯ A B

Bm7 Second Inversion

F♯ A B D

Bm7 Third Inversion

A B D F♯

Bm(maj7) Root Position

B D F♯ A♯

Bm(maj7) First Inversion

D F♯ A♯ B

Bm(maj7) Second Inversion

F♯ A♯ B D

Bm(maj7) Third Inversion

A♯ B D F♯

B

B5

B7#9

Bmaj7#11

B9

Bmaj9

B11, B9(sus4)

B13

Bm9

Bm11